LEARNING TECHNOLOGY HOW INFLUENCES

FARMING DEVELOPMENT

JOHN LOK

Introduction

Social Psychology means the scientific study of how we feel about, think about, and behave towtard the people around us and how our feeling , thoughts and behaviors are influenced by those people. So, if businessmen can know social psychology, they can learn consumer behavior, even how consumer behavior can bring ther business growth in behavioral economic view. This book can explain how and why any kinds of businesses need to learn social psychology into order to help them to increase customers number when recession occurs to themselves countries.

Farming industry is important food industry, farming industry may include farming products and non-farming products, it may include: farming of wheat, fruit, meat,corn , cotton etc.food and non-food products. So, any countries governments and farmers ought need to concern how to learn farming technology to improve and help them to achieve farming economic development. In my this book, I shall attempt to explain what farming technology means and how learning farming technology can help any countries to bring economy growth , how raising farming and non-farming productivities to bring farmer individual profit methods.

I shall concentrate on research China and India and developing coutnries and developed countries, UK, US farming industry ought how to improve their faming technology in order to raise farming productivities. This book is suitable to any students like to learn what farming economy concept is and how farming technology ought to be improved to achieve farming products and non-farming products productivities.

In my this book, I shall attempt to indicate future farming development customer needs problems . I also apply demand and supply theory to explain the developed countries' low wage growth how to influence food quality demand . In my this book seond part, I shall explain farming development of global food quality demand why is similar to public transport , leisure broadcasting, oil industry consumer needs to be influenced by economic environment changes as well as general people income level changes.

Contents

Prologue

Table of content

Chapter 1

Introduction to farming industry development

Introduction to farming industry development

Learning agricultural economic advantages

What is agricultural economic? What is farming? Why do we need to learn agricultural economy? Farming is an organized way to produce food., bio-energy and other non-food foods by cultivation. Agricultural economies deals with how to organize other non-foods; how the products are distributed, handled and consumed; and with the local and global impact this has on living conditions, societies, environment and economies. Also, farming and argicultural economic has close relationship.When global farming development can be kept the best, then it will bring every farmer has good income, even the country's economy will be also improved.

Farming can be defined as an organized way to grow crops and rear animals in order to provide food, bio-energy and other non-foods through cultivation with the purpose of selling the products, or using them in kind. Our definition of farming includes all kinds of animal farming and plant farming everywhere, irrespective of location aims of production, methods of production, economy and society. It refers to all kinds of outdoor crop cultivation, plus greenhouse cultivation, and forms of animal food. We won't exclude fish farming. Farming activities include all kinds of form work that is conducted with or without the help of machinery and equipment, such as tractor driving control of automatic milking, field inspections, equipment repairs, digging ditches, mending fences, carrying feed and water for farm

animals, making budgets and discussion with agricultural advises. Finally, agriculture aovers a wider field than farming , for example in formulations , such as

agricultural production, agricultural sectors and politics.

Agriculture is whether a meeting between nature and human society? Whehter is necessary for human survival? Is it dependent on land, is ruled by weather, seasons and

biological rhythms, is both predictable and unpredictable, economizing with resources, is conducted by large numbers of farmers, and may be highly influenced by social and cultural factors? Why is agriculture both predictable and unpredictable? Because seasonality influences practical farming, agricultural business and food consumption. If the harvest fails, one generally has to wait for the right season before it is possible to start all cover again, for example, on grazing seasons. Seasonality thus characrerizes much of farm work and yearly rhythm in farming. So, the season may impacts supply and demand for agricultural products, and price levels on inputs as sowing seed, and outputs , such as grains and meats.Hence, farming's dependency on nature means that agriculture is both highly predictable and unpredictable. Days and seasons come and go, which gives farming a repetitive and foreseeable character. Both crop farming and livestock production are in ordinary weather patterns and seasons. Prolonged rainy seasons can delay seedinf and distrurb the entire growing season.

Why do farmers need to choose how to use degree of farming market orientation? Some kinds of farming are certainly much more frequent in some parts of the world trhan in others,for example, find both big commercial farms and poor smallholdings in Kenya, India, China and Braxil. There may also be homogenous farmung on plains where farmers have more in common with colleagues across border than with smallholders in other parts of the same country. So, China, INdia, Brazil and Kenya farmers need to choose where grow good taste food, fruit , vegetable in order to make wrong farming land investment loss.

What is food chain relationship? A food chain can be defined as a linear sequential structure that shows varios stages along the processes of production, handling and consumption of food. The food chain approach is widely applied, and a way to involve , such as the farmer, the transport sector and the consumer. It is also appliable to fibre, bio-energy and other non-food chains that are being produced in a agricultural sector. However, the chains for marketed foods is complex. On input supply hand, the purchased input resources that are put into the food chain. Among the input suppliers to farm production, such as fertilizer industries, seed companies, animal feed companies, farm machinery companies, agro-chemical industries,petrochemical companies and electricity suppliers. Energy and chemicals are also continuously required during later stages, which also use large amounts of inputs, such as packaging materials, transport and storage facilities. Then farmers are main the market oriented farm production of crops role and animal products, fibres, bio-energy and varying by-products form the basis for food chains and other agricultural chains role both.

The intermediate stages include larger or smaller parts of the total handling and final costs for agricultural product. SOme of these activities are frequently repeated along the chain, not least transport, repackaging and intermediate storeage. It includes these processes, such as post-harvest processes, storage , transport, distribution, wholesale, food processing, such as change and/or preserve foods, packaging and retailing. The final stage is consumption , or eating, it relates to consumer individual food purchase choice activities, such as the trip to the supermarket, storing in the household and cooking, and eventually alos some care with packaging and food waste.

However, waste is produced all along the chain, and is a by-products to foods. The distination between waste and by-products may be a some that to a great extent is decided by the ambition to reuse or recycle. Nonetheless, waste occurs, stored in landfills and/or emitted into air and water. Consequently, waste can cause air and water pollution to our natural environment. For example, HOng Kong city is not a good place to develop farming industry. The reasons may include: air and water is polluted seriously, the numebr of people living in urban areas had exceed the number of people in countryside in Hong Kong city, due to population had been increasing from Chinese emmigrants every day. Hence, HOng KOng';s agriculture development is worse and difficult to compare prior 1960. Moreover, HOng JOng has many people need to live, so many lands had been using to build houses, because HOng KOng is a small city, land shortage is serious. So, shortage of land supply and ships' gas emission and cars' fuels pollutes Hong KOng seas, rivers, and air. Hence, these HOng Kong

people's activities, manufacturers' pollution activites on manufacturing processes, shipping transport's oil emission activities , even air planes flying activities had influenced Hong KOng can not provide good natural environment to carry on farming activities in order to grow up its agricultural economic development again easily after 1960. Also, it means that Hong KOng's land used for permanent crops won't have possible to develop again. It is HOng KOng government's duty. It only considers housing, financial activities aspect, but it neglects to research how to continue to develop its farming activities in order to bring agricultural economic growth, such as before 1960's successful agricultural development on rural.

Why do we need to know where can provide enough livestosk food to eat and good climate environment farming land use? The reason is simple, global population is continue increasing, such as China, India. They are increasing many people , they feel needs to live in themselves countries, if they can not know how to find the best farming lands to grow food, vegetables , fruits

or let livestock to alive. Then, the future food shortage challenges may occur to cause these countries have many people die because global has no enough foods to supply to them to eat in possible. So, studies of farm animals around the world teach is to the most varied types of landscapes and places, such as windblown moorlands, muddy backyards and enornous pigs or chickens, plants. SOme of kinds of animal farming are based on vast land areas, such as nomadism and large-scale rearing of sheep or cattle on low yielding pastures.

IN constrast, scientists find increasing numbers of plants with tens of thousands of pigs or chickens, to which the feed is transported from far away. So, seeking the best farming lands will be needed to any countries farmers in order to raise farming foods productive number more easily. The lands have enough water, none dry weater. Then, the land will be a good farming or harrested more easily. Farmers also need to know how to solve environmental problems to influence various kinds of livestock production.

They may include (1) how to directly connected with animals, such as emissions of greenhouse gases, such as carbon dioxide and methane from ruminants; emissions of nitrous oxide from animal manure; overgrazing, causing soil erosion and reduced biodiversity; leakage of nutrients from animal manure into water courses, high consumption of water, especially by high producing dairy cattles. (2) connected with feed production, it may include: Emissions of greenhouse, gases due to methods of cultivation; ;and degraduation due to eventual exploitation of forests and permanent pastures; problems due to use; overuse; of fertilizer and pesticides; water problems due to irrigation of feed crops, (3) connected with other parts of the food chain, it may include: Emissions from transportation, cooling, processing and packaging along the animal food chain.

Current trends in global livestock production need must increase. The reasons may include that the world has experienced large-scale increases in demand food of animal origin , when increased world population, increased per capita consumption of animal foods, increased livestock production need, partly on the basis of highly resource intensive methods of production, increased attention to the livestock sector's negative impact on climate change, increased attention to the livestock sector's negative impact on other environmental problems, increased attention to the value of animal

production for reducing poverty and generating cash income and developing smallholder farming needs.

Another learning agricultural economic reason, instead of solution to above farming land shortage and environment pollution influences difficult growing foods reason. The reason is learning how to increase agricultural production of non-foods. Agricultural non-food production includes all kinds of products that are obtained through farming for other purposes than to be eaten. Dealing with agricultural non-food production includes a plathre of different activites, such as : production of commodities, utilization of by-products, recycling of organic matter, various agricultural related service and extraaction of bio-energy.

Bearing in mind, that one-third of the global land area is agricultural land(plus another one-third of forest land), farming is involved in flows of energy and i ncontinuous growth of enormous quantities of organic substances in the form of vegetable and animal matter. This gives thew agricultural sector a unique position in the border land between agriculture, energy and other natural resources. IN this perspective, human may perceive the farmed landscape as an area for the production with more or less ambitious utilization of by-products and recycling of resources plus numerous other beneficial activities. For example, natural fibes from crop and other plants contribute to substantial parts of the entire agricultural non-food production. For another example, in cotton farming, connon lint is ususally the main purpose, with cotton seed as by-product , although both are highly valuable. Other plant fibes are of more typical by-product character. COir fibes from coconuts, for another example, are quite useful for mats and brushes, but hardly the primary motive for coconut production. IN addition, fibre crops generate straw and husks at early stages of the fibre chains and further along the chains other fibrous residues may be achieved. SOme of these may be used in animal husbandry, as building material or compested to be cycled back into the land. At the same time as some of the traditional use of fibres is replaced by plastics, new fields of application are being developed , such as mixtures between natural and synthetic fibes for industrial purposes.

However, cotton is globally traded and an important commodity in the world economy with regard to both the fibres and its valuable oil and protein rich cotton seed. IN addition, cotton is also important at regional and local levels, like many other plant fibres. According to FAOSTAT, the largeest amount of cotton lint was in 2009 produced by China, with India , in second place, US in third and Pakistan as number four. Taken together, the four leading cotton producing countries allounteed for much as 72 per cent of the total quantity.

On conclusion, following above issues , they explain that learning agricultural economy can also help any countries' non-food farming production farming industry, instead of food farming production development. Hence, it will be our future any countries and farmers duties to learn how to develop agriculture in order to make the best choice to achieve the maximum non-farming food or farming food production to bring global human living benefits.

● Farming economy researchs

Agricultural economics, study of the allocation, distribution, and utilization of the resources used, along with the commodities produced, by farming. Agricultural economics plays a role in the economics of development, for a continuous level of farm surplus is one of the wellsprings of technological and commercial growth.

Farmers have always had to worry about economics. At what price can they sell their produce? Will buying new dairy cows pay off in having more milk to sell? What's the going rate for farm labor? However, agricultural economics, meaning establishing general principles and scientific rules to answer such questions, didn't develop until the late 19th or early 20th century.While some economists focus on theory, the importance of agricultural economics is that it's an applied discipline, not just academic.

Farmers need information that helps them stay afloat financially, and the various types of agricultural economics tackle the relevant issues. In general, one can say that when a large fraction of a country's population depends on agriculture for its livelihood, average incomes are low. That does not mean that a country is poor because most of its population is engaged in agriculture; it is closer to the truth to say that because a country is poor, most of its people must rely upon agriculture for a living.

In general, farmers and economists will like to resesrch these questions or concern these questions when farmers grow their farming business or farming economist research how farming industry brings our global economic influences, these questions may include: What are the production costs of agriculture? How can farmers manage them successfully? How can farmers use their land and their workforce most effectively? Do the costs of buying equipment outweigh the profits of greater mechanized efficiency? As demands change, such as the growing interest in organic produce, is it necessary or profitable for farmers to change what they grow or how they produce it? How can society balance the needs of farmers with those of hikers, dirt bikers and other outdoor-recreation enthusiasts? How do we balance the needs of farmers with the needs of the environment? What should government farm policy entail? etc. different questions. For example, if a family's income were to increase by 100 percent, the amount it would spend on food might increase by 60 percent; if formerly its expenditures on food had been 50 percent of its budget, after the increase they would amount to only 40 percent of its budget. It follows that as incomes increase, a smaller fraction of the total resources of society is required to produce the amount of food demanded by the population.

How farming industry develops ? That fact would have surprised most economists of the early 19th century, who feared that the limited supply of land in the populated areas of Europe would determine the continent's ability to feed its growing population. Their fear was based on the so-called law of diminishing returns:

that under given conditions an increase in the amount of labour and capital applied to a fixed amount of land results in a less-than-proportional increase in the output of food. That principle is a valid one, but what the classical economists could not foresee was the extent to which the state of the arts and the methods of production would change. Some of the changes occurred in agriculture; others occurred in other sectors of the economy but had a major effect on the supply of food.

In looking back upon the history of the more developed countries, one can see that agriculture has played an important part in the process of their enrichment. For one thing, if development is to occur, agriculture must be able to produce a surplus of food to maintain the growing nonagricultural labour force. Since food is more essential for life than are the services provided by merchants or bankers or factories, an economy cannot shift to such activities unless food is available for barter or sale in sufficient quantities to support those engaged in them. Unless food can be obtained through international trade, a country does not normally develop industrially until its farm areas can supply its towns with food in exchange for the products of their factories.

Economic development also requires a growing labour force. In an agricultural country most of the workers needed must come from the rural population. Thus agriculture must not only supply a surplus of food for the towns, but it must also be able to produce the increased amount of food with a relatively smaller labour force. It may do so by substituting animal power for human power or by gradually introducing labour-saving machinery.

Agriculture may also be a source of the capital needed for industrial development to the extent that it provides a surplus that may be converted into the funds needed to purchase industrial equipment or to build roads and provide public services. For those reasons, a country seeking to develop its economy may be well advised to give a significant priority to agriculture. Experience in the developing countries has shown that agriculture can be made much more productive with the proper investment in irrigation systems, research, fertilizers, insecticides, and herbicides.

Like many economic disciplines, the agricultural economics definition stretches to a wide variety of fields and career paths. Agribusiness addresses issues in marketing, farm management, agricultural finance and trade. Policy analysts look at the effect of government agricultural policy on farms. Market researchers study market conditions to gauge the sales potential of different farm products. So, farming economic may include these aspects of research

1 Rural development and regional economics

2 Supply chain study and management

3 Natural resource economics, which studies how farmers can get the maximum use out of their land and other resources

4 Risk analysis

● Factors may bring risks to any farmers.

1 Time and Change external environment factor

Farming has always had an element of risk: One bad harvest or a crop blight can ruin a farm. However, the economics have changed over the centuries. At one time, increasing farm production was done entirely by expanding the amount of agricultural land: double the size of the farm, double the yields. Now, however, land is harder to come by, so farmers rely more on high-yield crops, machinery and the use of fertilizer. Another change is that governments in the 20th century became much more involved in controlling prices for produce. Agricultural prices fluctuate due to yield, supply and demand, so stabilizing prices and ensuring that farmers stay in business became a government priority.

2 Economic Factors Affecting Farming

Although farming is one of the world's oldest professions, modern farming is affected by uniquely modern economic factors. Farmers today compete in a complex economic environment where customers choose from produce grown all over the world and governments provide financial incentives for the production of certain crops rather than others. Although independently minded growers manage to create markets of their own through direct sales and other creative strategies, the majority of American farmers are still at the mercy of both economic factors and the weather.

Commodity Prices

The price of major commodity crops such as corn and soy depends of a variety of factors, such as investor speculation, weather and demand for these crops for both food and nonfood uses such as biofuels. Farmers who grow commodity crops earn or lose money based on the current rate that industrial buyers will pay for their output. In addition, commodity prices are affected by international economic factors, such as the weakness or strength of the dollar, because these farmers are competing with American farmers as well as with growers from all over the world.

Subsidies

The American government pays subsidies to farmers who grow commodity crops such as corn and soy because modern federal agricultural policy is based on the assumption that agricultural mass production benefits the economy by keeping food prices low. In theory, this policy provides farmers with a measure of economic stability, and provides consumers with affordable prices on the many processed food products made from these commodity crops. This policy encourages farmers to create an oversupply of a narrow range of crops because they make money for growing these foods regardless of current market conditions.

Labor and Immigration Laws

For better or for worse, mainstream agriculture depends on poorly paid labor that is often performed by migrant farmers, who are frequently living in the country illegally. The work pays so little that most naturally born citizens are unwilling to do it. If we are to continue buying agricultural produce at the prices to which we have grown accustomed, we must rely on workers who will work for the low wages that are customary in the field. Farming is affected by immigration laws that influence the availability of labor, as well as labor laws that allow or disallow subsistence agricultural wages.

What risks and opportunities corn or cotton farmers need to concern ? The cotton industry is huge, with cotton grown in dozens of countries around the world. Becoming a cotton farmer on a small scale is easier than starting a commercially viable farm that can compete with the enormous operations that already control the market. Cotton is a crop that requires lots of hot weather, so it is only viable in southern locations. Buy land that is suitable for growing cotton. corn farmer will need a location with a lot of hot, sunny weather and access to water. If a corn farmer is growing cotton as a hobby or for personal use, his farm doesn't need to be very large. If the corn farmer is attempting to make a living as a cotton farmer, he will need to profit from economies of scale, and will require at least 100 acres of land. This can be done on the job by working on a cotton farm and how operate the cotton plant, or more formally by attending an agricultural college and pursuing an advanced degree in agriculture. Learning by trial and error can be an expensive proposition in agriculture; the more the corn farmer learns in advance from the experience of others, the more likely the corn farmer is to avoid expensive mistakes. Plant the cotton farmer cotton seeds and provide them with all the requirements for them to thrive, including fertile soil, water and sunshine. Conventional cotton growing involves the use of large amounts of pesticides and herbicides. Decide if this the route what the cotton farmer wants to pursue, or if he wants to attempt to grow organic cotton. Growing organically is more labor-intensive, but the cotton farmer can sell his crop at a higher price. Develop a working relationship with suppliers and buyers. Agriculture is a competitive business, and any cotton farmers will need connections and a good reputation to sell their crop every year for a good price.

What are fish farming risks and opportunities ? Fish farming is a hot topic in some circles. Environmentalists are often critical of the impact fish farms can have on the environment, while advocates point out that they're a crucial source of high-quality protein. Wherever fish farmers stand on that debate, one of the big advantages of fish farming is that it's a fine entrepreneurial opportunity.

The Fundamental Problem which any fish farmers will be possible to encounter, they may include: Fish farming exists to address a fundamental problem, the demand for fish as a food source grows as the human population grows, and the number of fish available in the wild isn't keeping pace. Even in carefully managed wild fisheries, the combination of climate change, pollution and pressure from fishermen can produce unpredictable variations in the supply of fish. In a worst-case scenario, that can cause a fish population to crash, as Atlantic cod did in the 1970s and 1980s. In the long term, expecting conventional fisheries to continue to meet the world's needs with wild fish is as unrealistic as expecting a network of hunters to keep supermarket meat cases filled. Fish farming, or aquaculture as it's formally known, will need to make up the difference.

Fish farming risk

1 Keeps Fish Affordable

One of the basic principles of economics is that if demand is increasing and the supply is not, costs will go up. Over time, that trend could make fish unaffordable for all but the affluent. Bucking that trend is one of the biggest advantages of fish farming. By providing a steady, reliable, high-volume supply of fish, it helps the price remain manageable for most shoppers.

2 Reliable Supply and Wide Distribution

Having a reliable supply of fish is another advantage of aquaculture. The wild fishery fluctuates naturally, with catches rising or falling by the day, month or season. Fish farms turn out predictable harvests of fish at consistent sizes, making it easy for chefs, supermarkets, fishmongers and individual customers to plan their purchases. For restaurants and processors, this consistency means they can easily provide portions in standard sizes, too. Another advantage of fish farming is that it brings the supply of fish to where the consumers are. From open pens in inland lakes to tanks and ponds on dry land, fish farms can be set up almost anywhere there's a market. This cuts the financial and environmental cost of shipping and provides consumers with fresher fish. That's a win-win.

3 Consumer Health

Health authorities worldwide encourage more fish consumption, including the USDA's Dietary Guidelines for Americans, because it's a high-quality protein source that's low in saturated fat. Salmon has the added advantage of being especially high in omega-3 fatty acids, which promote heart health. Switching just a few meals per week from red meat to fish is not only healthier as a dietary choice, it's environmentally friendly as well: Fish farming is generally "greener" than meat production.

4 Preserves Wild Stocks

Another advantage of aquaculture is its potential to reduce the strain on wild fisheries and native fish stocks. The more fish farming meets our needs, the less incentive there is to purchase wild-caught fish. That in turn reduces the temptation to overfish and improves the likelihood that wild stocks can maintain a healthy population. Immature fish bred in captivity can even be used to re-establish species in places where they've been wiped out by overfishing. However, one frequent criticism of fish farms is that they're not always efficient providers of dietary protein. Some operations rely on wild-caught "trash" fish or bait fish for much of their feed, meaning it's quite possible for the fish to consume more protein than they produce.

5 Risk to Wild Stocks

Unfortunately, fish farming also poses a risk to wild fish populations. Open-pen fish farms concentrate the creatures at unnaturally high levels, increasing waste and the risk of disease, just as many land-based hog and chicken farms do. This poses a threat to wild fish, which can be infected. Inland fresh-water systems can be just as harmful if they're located in a lake or river with its own wild species. Land-based systems that return used water to the local watershed also pose some risk. Escaped fish from these pens can become invasive, as fast-growing carp and tilapia do inland or farmed Atlantic salmon do on the West Coast.

6 Fish Farming as Entrepreneurial Opportunity

One additional advantage of fish farming is that it represents an opportunity from which entrepreneurs almost anywhere can benefit. Farms can be situated anywhere from open coastlines to a farmer's "back 40" to a shuttered factory in a Rust Belt city. Startup costs can be surprisingly low for a small operation, largely a matter of choosing the right species to cultivate and providing a suitable environment. Salmon, trout, catfish, tilapia, shrimp and crawfish are all common options. Some operators maximize their productivity through composite fish culture, which is raising a combination of compatible, noncompetitive species in the same bodies of water. This gives you more variety in your product line and more fish to sell at little additional cost.

● How economic Impact to fish and cotton farming industries

The social science of economics began as a branch of philosophy, but emerged as a separate discipline in the late 18th century after the publication of Adam Smith's landmark work, "The Wealth of Nations." Since then, economics has provided a scientific approach to understanding the ways in which families, firms and entire societies allocate resources to satisfy their needs and wants.

People live in a world of scarcity in which all resources—time, money, land and others—are finite. Because people do not have unlimited resources, they must allocate their time, money and other resources in a way that will achieve as many of their needs and wants as possible. For example, consumers want to obtain maximum value for their money, and businesses want to maximize profits subject to their existing capacity for production. Economics provides a systematic way to study production, consumption and resource allocation.

Throughout history, people have dealt with issues of resource allocation; often human survival depended on it. The concept of an economy did not develop until the Middle Ages, although markets and trade have existed since ancient times. Until the era of the Enlightenment in the 18th century, economics was not a discipline of its own, but a branch of philosophy, which also examined political, ethical and religious issues.Just as biologists and chemists apply scientific methods to understand questions involving biological and chemical phenomena, economists employ scientific methods, including hypothesis testing and quantitative analysis, to understand and explain economic phenomena. Why apartment rents are so much higher in New York City than in Austin, Texas; how government monetary policy will affect retail prices; what factors affect average wages in different countries—these and other questions involve economic phenomena. As a science, economics strives to provide answers and explanations.

Hence, economics plays an important role in the analysis and formulation of government policy. Just as consumers want maximum value for their money, politicians and taxpayers want to maximize the value of their taxes and other government resources at the lowest cost. Economists have an important voice in the policy arena, helping identify the types of policies that maximize benefits at the least cost to the public.As a scientific approach to policy, economics not only informs the debate over issues related to taxation, government spending and economic policies; it also applies to the full range of public policy issues, including health care, defense, education, energy and the environment.

Catfish Farming How Bring Profit

If one fish farmer or cotton farmer is looking for a decisive argument in favor of aquaculture, simple economics can provide one. The U.S. imports over 90 percent of its seafood, creating a yearly trade deficit that the USDA's Agricultural Research Service estimated at $14 billion as of January 2018. When you combine that economic impact with a fish farm's ability to fit in almost anywhere, the potential is clear: Fish or cotton farming can produce economic growth in places where jobs are sorely needed. Managing a fish or cotton farm sustainably can help reduce its disadvantages and increase its advantages. For conventional open-pen operators, for example, that can mean reducing the populations of fish or cotton in each pen to cut down on waste and reduce the need for medications. On land, fish or cotton farmers can opt for recirculating aquaculture systems that filter and reuse the same water constantly, isolating the farmed fish from local waterways and minimizing the risk that they'll escape and become invasive.

An especially appealing option is aquaponics, a method of growing vegetable crops such as herbs, lettuce and tomatoes hydroponically with the same water that supports the fish. Waste from the fish fertilizes the plants, which in turn helps filter the water and keeps the fish healthy.

Aquaculture dates back thousands of years ago and is now a rapidly expanding business practice in the United States. Operating a catfish farm, for example, requires a precise and well-executed business plan. Farm operators must raise large amounts of capital to even begin a small fish-farming practice. There are, however, many benefits to fish farming over cattle or chicken farming, and savvy business considerations can help you how to profit in the world of farming catfish. For example, invest in a large farm. Large farms, on one hand, demand more acreage, thus costing more money. A farm costing $5,000 per acre multiplied by 90 acres equals $450,000 in the initial investment of the pond property alone. Building a large farm, however, allows you to sell more fish at one time — substantially increasing profit margins over smaller farms. Moreover, larger farms can export more easily to international markets — such as Asia — where fish is widely consumed. Design fish farm in a location with moderate temperatures and geography. Climates with excessive rain or snow can damage fish farming with flooding or freezing water. Choosing a geographical location away from areas where fault lines, tornadoes or hurricanes can result in annual natural disasters is also wise for the preservation of fish farm.Sell fishes in direct sales. Selling catfish direct to market eliminates the costs of unnecessary business entities raising the cost and taking a cut of the profits before the product reaches the consumer. Direct sales to a processing factory — which then sells directly to the public — reduce the need for dealing with grocery store chains or other costly business outlets. Using direct sales is a way to keep consumer prices down, maintain the freshness in fish and sell more of the product at one time.

● Pros and Cons of Biotechnology in Agriculture

If most people had to list the disadvantages of biotechnology, agricultural uses would rank high. Just look at how many foods proudly advertise as having no genetically modified ingredients. What are the advantages and disadvantages of biotechnology in agriculture?

Consider the pros of biotechnology, they may include:

Genetically engineering crops can make them resistant to disease and insect attacks. Inserting genes that make crops immune to herbicide allows farmers to eliminate weeds without hurting crops. There's less need to till the soil to kill weeds, which reduces erosion. Plants can produce toxic chemicals that kill off insect predators. Genetic engineering can make plants produce more food or improve their nutritional profile. Biotechnology can keep plant foods shelf-stable for longer periods.

Consider the cons of biotechnology they may include:

As farmers use herbicides more regularly, it accelerates the development of immunity in weeds. Genetically modified organisms are covered by patents. Farmers who replant seeds from a patented crop as they would with ordinary plants have faced lawsuits. Relying on GMOs reduces the natural genetic diversity found in agriculture. If, say, all corn or soybeans have the same genetic profile, there's a greater chance of some fungus or parasite wiping out the entire national crop. GMO seed is more expensive, though it can also lead to greater profits from a larger yield.

Risks of Biotechnology in Humans

Many people are uneasy about having products from GMOs in their food. Genetic engineering in human beings raises even more concern about the negative aspects of biotechnology. Monstrous experiments on humans have been a staple of horror movies, and for many people, the real thing is equally as troubling.

Many diseases stem from genetic problems, so treating them genetically can save or transform lives. This is effective if there's a single genetic issue that's easy to identify and treat. It's possible that eventually, we will be able to enhance human beings: stronger hearts, greater intelligence, more disease resistance. Much of our bodies and health aren't the product of single genes but complex interactions. It's entirely possible that in trying to improve ourselves, we'll create unwanted, disastrous side effects.

Some genetic diseases aren't as simple to treat as fixing one rogue gene. There are serious ethical issues when science experiments on humans. If we're altering genes to "improve" people, does that raise different ethical questions from altering genes to fix verifiable problems? Can we regulate human biotechnological treatments to gain benefits while restricting abuse?

All of above biotechnology technology whether it ought to apply to any agriculture industry to bring advantages and disadvantges, any farmers or farming economists or agricultural scientists must need to evaluate whether what future negative or positive influences human will face.

CHAPTER TWO

How developing countries develop farming industry

● How India land supply shortage may influence India farming industry economic development

We know how agriculture contributes to economic development and then how industry contributes towards development. However, the issue of choice of one sector over the other remains unresolved as far as economic policy is concerned. Industry which is, no doubt, important, will not progress unless agriculture is sound, stable, and progressive. Because of this interdependence these sectors are complementary, and not competitive. In the development of an underdeveloped economy, there is as such no conflict between agricultural and industrial development.

Hence, interdependence between agriculture and industry becomes strengthened through various linkages generated in these two sectors. The three most important linkages are : production linkages, demand linkages, and saving-investment linkages.Production linkages arise from the interdependence between agriculture and industry through the use of productive inputs. Agriculture draws some raw materials, like chemical fertilisers, pesticides, electric power, agricultural machinery and implements, etc., from the industry. Agriculture is also dependent on industry for the supply of materials for building up social and economic overheads in the agricultural sector. Further, many raw materials and inputs used in industrial production, e.g., cotton, jute, sugarcane, tobacco, etc., is supplied by the agricultural sector.

Demand linkages between the two sectors suggest that demand for one sector's product pulls demand for another sector in an upward direction. Urbanisation and industrialisation are synonymous. Under the impact of Green Revolution, agriculturists now experience rising rural incomes which has brought a change in the pattern of tastes and preferences of rural people. Increased rural income has resulted in an entry of industrial consumer goods, like TV, refrigerator, modem, car, footwear, refined sugar, edible oils, motorbikes, etc. In the urban areas, we see some sort of demand saturation of some of these products of consumer goods industries. The impact of rising urban incomes and industrialisation has a favourable impact on the demand for food, vegetables, fruits, various raw materials produced in the agricultural sector. It has been an article of faith in India that the demand stimulus for industrial expansion would likely come mainly from agriculture with low social and economic costs.

Finally, there is a savings-investment linkage between these two sectors. A self-reliant agriculture capable of exporting surplus food-grains helps in saving scarce foreign exchange resources of the country. Now these resources can be better utilised for importing capital goods and crucial raw materials needed for industrialisation effort. As agricultural production and productivity rises above the subsistence requirement, the volume of marketable surplus increases which provides sinews of industrialisation, particularly in the rural sector. Again, the rising volume of savings and capital formation consequent upon rising farm incomes give strong stimulus to demand for manufactured goods. Investment in one sector pulls investment of other sectors up thereby accelerating overall growth rate of the economy.

Similarly, the rise in non-farm incomes leads to an increase in the demand for various agricultural products. In the process, agricultural sector becomes diversified, modernised. Most importantly, the relative terms of trade between the two sectors affect the flow of resources from one to another sector. Terms of trade will improve for agricultural sector if over a period of time the prices of agricultural commodities move at a higher rate than the prices of manufactured articles. Thus, the terms of trade favouring agriculture results in an increased real income and hence, increased private saving and investment. The relative terms of trade also influence government saving and investment in these two sectors.If technological change is made in the primary sector there will be more surplus and, hence, more output in the industrial sector.

In the end, we must say a few words about the problem of inter-sectoral resource allocation. To begin with, it is almost impossible to make an optimum balance between these two sectors. In many of the developing countries, agriculture no longer enjoys a pride of place, for some obvious reasons. Neo-liberal era has seen the over-emphasis on the urban, industrial sector. That is why agricultural land is now being forcibly taken away for industrial development, infrastructural developments, and so on. Against this backdrop, farmers of these economies have been shifting their attention from the agricultural sector towards non- agricultural activities. How far these two sectors will complement each other, and to what degree, is an important issue. Indeed, the failure on the agriculture front is of tern attributed to faulty agricultural policy in many developing countries, including India. So, India is one good farming industry needing developing country example, any India fish and corn , furit , wheat, rice and meat farmers must need to concern how to use land natural resource for their farming development in order to avoid farming lands shorage challenge to influence India farming industry economic development.

- The Relationship between Economic Growth and Agricultural Growth To China

What is agricultural industry policy to future China ? China is number one in Agriculture. China ranks first in worldwide farm output, primarily producing rice, wheat, potatoes, tomato, sorghum, peanuts, tea, millet, barley, cotton, oilseed, corn and soybeans. The development of farming over the course of China's history has played a key role in supporting the growth of what is now the largest population in the world. Analysis of stone tools by Professor Liu Li and others has shown that hunter-gatherers 23,000–19,500 years ago ground wild plants with the same tools that would later be used for millet and rice.

What is China Farming method improvements ? Due to China's status as a developing country and its severe shortage of arable land, farming in China has always been very labor-intensive. However, throughout its history, various methods have been developed or imported that enabled greater farming production and efficiency. They also utilized the seed drill to help improve on row farming. For agricultural purposes the Chinese had invented the hydraulic-powered trip hammer by the 1st century BC. Although it found other purposes, its main function was to pound, decorticate, and polish grain that otherwise would have been done manually. The Chinese also innovated the square-pallet chain pump by the 1st century AD, powered by a waterwheel or oxen pulling on a system of mechanical wheels. Although the chain pump found use in public works of providing water for urban and palatial pipe systems, it was used largely to lift water from a lower to higher elevation in filling irrigation canals and channels for farmland.

Since 1994, the government has instituted a number of policy changes aimed at limiting grain importation and increasing economic stability. Among these policy changes was the artificial increase of grain prices above market levels. This has led to increased grain production, while placing the heavy burden of maintaining these prices on the government. In 1995, the "Governor's Grain Bag Responsibility System" was instituted, holding provincial governors responsible for balancing grain supply and demand and stabilizing grain prices in their provinces. Later, in 1997, the "Four Separations and One Perfection" program was implemented to relieve some of the monetary burdens placed on the government by its grain policy. As China continues to industrialize, vast swaths of agricultural land is being converted into industrial land. Farmers displaced by such urban expansion often become migrant labor for factories, but other farmers feel disenfranchised and cheated by the encroachment of industry and the growing disparity between urban and rural wealth and income. The most recent innovation in Chinese agriculture is a push into organic agriculture. This rapid embrace of organic farming simultaneously serves multiple purposes, including food safety, health benefits, export opportunities, and, by providing price premiums for the produce of rural communities, the adoption of organics can help stem the migration of rural workers to the cities.In the mid-1990s China became a net importer of grain, since its unsustainable practises of groundwater mining has effectively removed considerable land from productive agricultural use. Due to China's status as a developing country and its severe shortage of arable land, farming in China has always been very labor-intensive. However, throughout its history, various methods have been developed or imported that enabled greater farming production and efficiency. They also utilized the seed drill to help improve on row farming.

However, China's agricultural productivity grew rapidly following the implementation of a series of economic reforms since 1978. Reforms led to more efficient resource allocation. China also began to disseminate new technologies (including improved seed varieties and animal breeds) and encourage mechanization. These "agricultural modernization" efforts laid a broad foundation for improved agricultural productivity. But evidence suggests that this growth may not continue into the future. With about 20 percent of the world's population, 6.5 percent of its land area, and rising living standards, China's ability to improve farm productivity will have a direct bearing on global food markets. China is already the leading importer of soybeans and cotton and has recently emerged as an importer of other major commodities, including corn, pork, wheat, and rice. A slowdown in productivity growth could bring further demand for imports.

During 1985-2007, China's agricultural output growth (in real terms) averaged 5.1 percent annually. Two developments underlie this growth: greater use of inputs and growth in what economists call "total factor productivity" (TFP), or the ability to produce more output from each unit of input. TFP growth contributed 2.7 percentage points to the growth in China's agricultural output while rising use of inputs contributed 2.4 percentage points. The mix of inputs changed as use of intermediate goods (including energy, pesticides, fertilizer, seed, feed, and other materials) grew 6.4 percent annually, offsetting declines in the use of labor and land. China's roughly equal reliance on increased input use and TFP contrasts with the recent experience of developed countries where TFP accounts for nearly all growth in agricultural output. For example, annual growth in U.S. agricultural TFP contributed 1.22 percentage points while input growth contributed 0.03 percentage points to output growth over 1985-2007. Future China farming productivities may include below several aspects:

1 Crop distribution

Although China's agricultural output is the largest in the world, only 10% of its total land area can be cultivated. China's arable land, which represents 10% of the total arable land in the world, supports over 20% of the world's population.[23] Of this approximately 1.4 million square kilometers of arable land, only about 1.2% (116,580 square kilometers) permanently supports crops and 525,800 square kilometers are irrigated.[citation needed] The land is divided into approximately 200 million households, with an average land allocation of just 0.65 hectares, China is the leading producer of cotton, which is grown throughout, but especially in the areas of the North China Plain, the Yangtze river delta, the middle Yangtze valley, and the Xinjiang Uygur Autonomous Region. Other fiber crops include ramie, flax, jute, and hemp. Sericulture, the practice of silkworm raising, is also practiced in central and southern China.

2 Livestock

China has a large livestock population, with pigs and fowls being the most common. China's pig population and pork production mainly lie along the Yangtze River. In 2011, Sichuan province had 51 million pigs (11% of China's total supply).[30] In rural western

China, sheep, goats, and camels are raised by nomadic herders.[31] In Tibet, yaks are raised as a source of food, fuel, and shelter. Cattle, water buffalo, horses, mules, and donkeys are also raised in China, and dairy has recently been encouraged by the government, even though approximately 92.3% of the adult population is affected by some level of lactose intolerance. As demand for gourmet foods grows, production of more exotic meats increases as well. Based on survey data from 684 Chinese turtle farms (less than half of the all 1,499 officially registered turtle farms in the year of the survey, 2002), they sold over 92,000 tons of turtles (around 128 million animals) per year; this is thought to correspond to the industrial total of over 300 million turtles per year. Increased incomes and increased demand for meat, especially pork, has resulted in demand for improved breeds of livestock, breeding stock imported particularly from the United States. Some of these breeds are adapted to factory farming.

3 Fishing

China accounts for about one-third of the total fish production of the world. Aquaculture, the breeding of fish in ponds and lakes, accounts for more than half of its output. The principal aquaculture-producing regions are close to urban markets in the middle and lower Yangtze valley and the Zhu Jiang delta.

● What risks China will encounter to farming industry

All of China's regions have experienced strong growth in agricultural production since the mid-1980s fueled by both input and TFP growth, but the relative contribution of these two factors differs by region. Provinces with the most rapid TFP growth include a mix of coastal regions that led China's economic development and several western provinces. Most northeastern and northern provinces exhibited more input growth. Although the growing economy has pulled labor and land away from farming, the development of China's nonfarm sectors may have benefited farming by generating funds for investment in public infrastructure, science, and technology. Relaxed restrictions on foreign trade and investment may also have enhanced agricultural productivity by improving access to new technology and new markets.

However, the rapid growth in the past few decades may not have been sustained in recent years. Annual TFP growth peaked during 1996-2000 at 5.1 percent before slowing to 3.2 percent in 2000-2005. It then declined by 3.7 percent per year in 2005-07. The significance of this slowdown remains unclear. It may reflect a turning point in China's agricultural productivity growth, in which case gains from earlier reforms and technology transfers from developed countries have been exhausted. Alternatively, it may simply be the effect of transitory events such as animal disease epidemics or discrepancies in data. As urbanization draws more labor and land from agriculture and accelerates changes in food consumption, the capacity to reestablish positive agricultural TFP growth is important to China's future. So, China needs to concerns below several aspects to raise itself farming industry competitive position to global farming competitive market.

1) Finance is emerging as a major driver of sustainability.

Government policy and consumer preferences can certainly shift corporate behaviour, as tariffs on soy have shown. And most consumer-facing businesses are adapting to their customers' preferences for more sustainability.

2) Innovation will be part of any solution.

While the public sector has limited funding resources, private investment and capability could play an instrumental role in achieving sustainable agricultural development goals. But current levels are not enough to meet global food security challenges in the long term. Private investors remain reluctant to invest in sustainable agriculture because of the perceived uncertainties and high risks. Furthermore, conventional financing models have their limits, particularly in developing countries where most of the growth in food demand and production will come from. China need more innovative financing in which public and private sectors can work together, to create the necessary policy and investment environment for private finance in sustainable farming. China also should look at the renewable energy sector for new ideas, where public-private partnerships (PPPs) have successfully delivered mechanisms for pooling public and private financing and risk mitigation. Chinese people may not like change, but they like innovation. People don't like to give things up, but they like to have new options. Innovation is the answer. It is essential to change.

3) Success depends on collaboration. Bringing people on board is a must. To identify a solution is much easier than to implement it. In theory, everybody wants a more sustainable food system. But not everybody wants or is able to pay the price. That's why sustainable change requires us to bring on board all those who are affected. In order to achieve a sustainable food chain, farmers and producers may need further incentives. China's sizeable Grain for Green project offered grains, tax and other encouragements so that farmers would protect, instead of clear, their forested slopes. And agribusinesses will be wise to adopt the same principle. Sustainable farming will only be possible if farmers are on board.

4) Success requires solutions at scale and China is well-placed to deliver them.

The urgency of our biodiversity and climate crises means that we need to have solutions in place right now. And these solutions need to be at scale. The sustainability-linked loan mentioned above is not the first in the agricultural trading sector, but it is the largest so far. It demonstrates our intention to join hands with others in our industry and to contribute to sustainable growth in the global agriculture sector. That is part of the Chinese dream.

Hence, all of above technological innovation is needed to developed to China future farm industry, if it still hope to raise farming competitive position in global farming market.

● What factors influence US farming development

In farming economic view, in general, these factors will influence any countries farming industry developement. They may include: Human factors that influence agricultural use include: Population size leads to larger areas of cultivation and competitio for land. Farming techniques. Final destination of production. Globalisation . Agricultural policies. Environmental policies aim to protect the environment and guarantee safe, healthy food. Social and economic factors. These are human factors and include labour, capital, technology, markets and government (political). These are physical factors and include climate, relief and soil. Temperature (minimum 6°C for crops to grow) and rainfall (at least 250mm to 500mm) influence the types of crops that can be grown, e.g. hot, wet tropical areas favour rice, while cooler, drier areas favour wheat. Although farming is one of the world's oldest professions, modern farming is affected by uniquely modern economic factors. Farmers today compete in a complex economic environment where customers choose from produce grown all over the world and governments provide financial incentives for the production of certain crops rather than others. Such as US is one developed country, whether what are the main factors to influence its farming industry development. I shall indicate these main factors as below:

The history of agriculture in the United States covers the period from the first English settlers to the present day. In Colonial America, agriculture was the primary livelihood for 90% of the population, and most towns were shipping points for the export of agricultural products. Most farms were geared toward subsistence production for family use. The rapid growth of population and the expansion of the frontier opened up large numbers of new farms, and clearing the land was a major preoccupation of farmers. After 1800, cotton became the chief crop in southern plantations, and the chief American export. After 1840, industrialization and urbanization opened up lucrative domestic markets. The number of farms grew from 1.4 million in 1850, to 4.0 million in 1880, and 6.4 million in 1910; then started to fall, dropping to 5.6 million in 1950 and 2.2 million in 2008.

Nowadays, US farming productivities may include :

Arable farming , it means growing of cereals, vegetables and animal feeds. Flat relief; fertile well-drained soils; warm summers; rainfall – under 650mm (some in growing season); winter frosts to break up soil and kill pestsPhysical factors Flat relief; fertile well-drained soils; warm summers; rainfall – under 650mm (some in growing season); winter frosts to break up soil and kill pests as well as Human factors. Large market in south east; good transport networks; benefits from US government subsidies and intervention price, they can influence US arable farming success.

Dairying, Rearing of cattle for milk. Hill sheep farming, sheep rearing for meat .Physical factors, Gentle relief; fertile soils; high rainfall for grass growth; mild winters (over 6°C).Human factors. Access to large markets; milk subsidies up to the 1980s when quotas introduce, they can influence US dairying development success.

Hill sheep farming.Wool and Market gardening, growing fruit, vegetables and flowers. Physical factors, High, steep relief; thin infertile soils; high rainfall (over 1000mm); low temperatures unsuitable for crops. Human factors, Remote from large markets; limited labour; EU subsidies and grants, they may influence hill sheep farming success.

Market gardening includes Growing fruit, vegetables and flowers. Physical factors, Long hours of sunshine; most other factors are controlled. Human factors, Access to motorways and airports; large labour and capital input. They may influence marketing gardening success.

There are these main factors still influence US future agricultural industry development as below:

On Human Factors aspect, it may include: Labour: All farms need either human labour or machinery to do the work. Some farm types use very little labour, e.g. sheep farming. Others require a large labour force, e.g. rice farming in India. Market: This is the customer who buys farm produce. Farmers need to sell their crops and animals to make a profit. Perishable crops such as soft fruits fetch a high price, but need to be grown with a short travelling distance of the market. Finance: Profits are used to pay the wages and to re-invest in the farm, e.g. buying seeds, fertiliser, machinery and animals. This is known as feedback within the farming system. Tradition: Farmers may have always farmed in a certain way and be unwilling to change. Politics: Government may provide subsidies and loans to encourage new farming practices but they may also place limits on production to prevent food surpluses, e.g. quotas and set-aside in the European Union.

On Physical Factors aspect, it may include: Climate: Temperature – a minimum temperature of 6°C is needed for crops to grow. The growing season is the number of months the temperature is over 6°C. Different crops need a different growing season, e.g. wheat needs 90 days. Rainfall – all crops and animals need water. Relief: Temperatures decrease by 1>°C every 160 metres vertical height. Uplands are more exposed to wind and rain. Steep slopes also cause thin soils and limit the use of machinery. Lowland areas are more easily farmed. Soils: Crops grow best on deep, fertile, free-draining soils, e.g. the brown earths found in lowland Britain. Less fertile soils prone to water logging are best used for pastoral farming. Geography Aspect: The direction a slope faces. South-facing slopes are best for growing crops.

Hence, environment and human, e.g. farmers, government, farming scientists etc. both will be main factors to influence US future farming industry development.

CHAPTER THREE

Learning future agricultural development is influenced by   technology

In consumer psychology and social psychology view is the study of dynamic relationship between individuals, (individual consumer) and the target of consumer group, e.g. young age, old age, male and female , income level etc. consumer target groups. Each of consumer is different, our consumer individual characteristics, including our personality traits, consumption desires, persuading consumption, motivations, and consumer individual, emotions, have an important impact on global consumer behavior. Consumer behavior evaluation may be calculated from consumer individual consumption desire and social environment consumption situation. The most basic tendancy of consumer motivation is the consumption desire to satisfy useful and enjoyment or leisure expectation on psychological satisfactory needs and useful needs to the kind of product or the kind of service.

Hence, it seems that of the businessmen can know whether the consumer whose real need to buy the kind of product, then he / she can raise sale price and sells the kinds of product more easily to compare his / her similar kinds of product sellers. However, consumer psychology and social psychology have close relationship in behavioral economic view. In general, social psychologists study real world problems using a scientific approach, consumer psychologists also seem to social psychologists to study real consumption world problems using a scientific approach.

Social psychology is based on affect (feelings), behavior (interactions) and cognition (thourht) interaction consumer psychology is also based on product affect (product useful satisfactory feelings) or leisure enjoyment feelings), be consumption behavior (using the product behavior or playing the kind of leisure behavior), using the product thought or playing the kind of leisure thought), why he / she feels need to use the product or why he / she feels need to play the leisure activity. Because in consumer psychology and social psychology view, they mean one explained that the sharing of goods, services, consumer individua enjoyment to the kind of leisure activity or using the kind of product emotions as well as external consumption environment of social outcomes is known as social consumption or social purchase and sale exchange. Social consumption rewards (the positive oucomes that businessmen give or sell the kind of products and receive purchase payment whom the kind of product businessmen interact with themselves cosusumers or product buyers), include social benefits as product sale income, consumer attention or consideration or hope to attempt to use the kind of product or play the kind of leisure activity, prise to product after using the kind of product. Consumer social cost may include the negative outcomes, when he / she feels dissatisfactory to use the kind of product or play the kinds of leisure activity on purchase payment loss.

So, any kinds of product sellers or leisure service providers need to learn how to maximize their easy sale outcomes by attempting to gain as many consumer social rewards as possible and by attempting to maximize consumers themselves consumption costs in order to excite consumers attempt to spend money to buy the product for using desire or play the leisure activity to enjoyment desire to compare whose similar kinds of sellers themselves products.

Finally, I shall indicate such as robots product example, in general car manufacturers will consider hoe they need to buy manufacturing robots in factory, they will consider manufacturing robots may help them to reduce how many workers number and wages in long term, how much car productive number and car manufacturing efficiencies robots can raise more than human workers, whether car manufacturing robots and human car manufacturing workers their skills whom can manufacture the most excellent kinds of cars to satisfy global car buyers needs, whether car manufacturing robots are often needed to repair when they are damaged easily in long term, they also will calculate between car manufacturing workers working emotion , negative feeling, tried, boring feeling psychological and physical problems and manufacturing robots repair problems, when the car manufacturer needs to make decision either to employ a number of car manufacturing workers or buy a number of car robots in the car manufacturing factory.

Hence, the car manufacturing robots seller needs to evaluate whether every potential car robot buyer purchase hoping, using hoping, using desire, e.g. what factors may encourage they choose to buy car manufacturing robots products to replace human car manufacturing workers,, what factors may influenece they forget to make car manufacture robots purchase decision, to replace human car manufacturing workers.

On conclusion, if this car manufacting robots seller ought attempt to learn car manufacture robots social and consumption psychology in global car manufacturing robots market, then it ought attempt to sell itself car manufacturing robots products to its potential car manufacturing robot customers more easily to compare its similar kinds of car manufacture robot competitors. Future agricultural food buyers their food choice purchase desires are also influenced by food technological influence. For wine example, if wine can be manufactured to improve wine taste by robot wine temperature control in wine store rooms, e.g. white or red wine can be kept in wine store rooms in the most suitable temperature to avoid wine bad taste casues easily. Then white and red wine buyers will choose to buy good taste white or red wine to drink in preference. So, future agricultural development is influenced by technological improvement.

* 9 7 9 8 8 8 9 3 5 2 6 4 8 *